5 Minute Mini-Sermons

D1738601

Pastor David Timothy

a.k.a. SoupMan

ISBN 9798536212387

10 9 8 7 6 5 4 3 2 1

Other Books by David Timothy

God is NEVER On Vacation!

Forged by Christ!

God is NOT on Vacation!

He Ain't no Billy Graham!

All of David's books are available at:

amazon.com

Publisher Note: David gives *all of his royalties* from his book sales to the SoupMobile to help feed the homeless & needy children. *He keeps nothing for himself.*

In Loving Memory of
Carroll Moran
Your Wings were Ready,
Our Hearts were Not!
9/22/64 – 12/11/20

TABLE OF CONTENTS

Dedication

I dedicate this book to my wife Shana, a.k.a. SoupGirl. She is nothing short of amazing! My life with her is terrific, fantastic, glorious, blissful, fun, dazzling, marvelous, splendid, wondrous, groovy & off the chain!

I consider her a blessing sent right from the Lord himself. Not just a blessing to me, but to her fellowman. Shana wears her heart on her sleeve and loves both people and animals.

The Lord has surely blessed me in life beyond anything I might deserve. God is soooooooooooooooooooooooo good!!!

Signed, David Timothy, a.k.a SoupMan

Author's Note

This book has 33 mini-Chapters, but if you were to read only #3 of them, I highly recommend Chapter's 0, 15 & 31. You may be asking? Can a book really have a Chapter 0? Well, not usually but in SoupLand, it can & does! May God bless & keep you!

**David & Shana were married on
October 18, 2008**

CHAPTER 0
BORING???

The book that you are holding in your hands is **not** your normal, by the numbers, within the margins type book. The book is actually a collection of **5 Minute Mini-Sermons** by Pastor David Timothy of SoupMobile Church. His flock call him the SoupMan, because he's served a lot of soup to the <u>homeless</u> & <u>needy children</u> in Dallas since the founding of the SoupMobile in **2003.**

My first thought when I heard this would be a book of Mini-Sermons was **BORING!** Really, a book of mini-sermons—did I mention **BORING!!!** But then I remembered who the Author of this book was, David Timothy, a guy who I hear is definitely **NOT** boring! He seems to walk to the beat of a different drummer, but he is quick to say that while his walk may be different, he doesn't think it's any better than anyone else's! If anything, David is humble and sometimes to a fault!

By the way, these mini-sermons aren't your regular stodgy, humdrum, dull, mind numbing, mundane & did I mention **BORING** type sermons. In fact, they are hard hitting, informative, even a bit of fun & YES, they can be a little out there! David covers everything from the Pandemic; Bette Davis; Mustard seeds; Donuts; Sharks; Mariah Carey; WarGames & oh yeah, a ton of really neat stuff about that Jesus guy!

How can I say all of this with such complete confidence & authority? How can I be so sure about this guy who walks to such a different

& unique beat??? Well, you see, I married this Non-boring, walks to a different beat drummer type guy and *I am the Pastor's wife!*

Signed, Shana Timothy
a.k.a. SoupGirl

----

p.s. These mini-sermons were birthed during the pandemic of 2020-21. Note that the sermons are in <u>no</u> particular date order & many of the statistics quoted in the sermons (particularly the number of Covid-19 cases & deaths) have <u>increased dramatically</u> since the sermons were written!

**The last known sighting
of a Dodo Bird was in
1662.**

1

Where is the Dodo Bird?

Some people may be scratching their heads and asking what's a Dodo bird? **Believe it or not the Dodo is a real bird**. However, it was a very unusual bird in that while it had wings it could <u>not</u> fly. It grew up to **4ft tall** and could weigh as much as **50 lbs.** The **Dodo** could only be found on the Island of Mauritius which is located in the Indian Ocean. While at one time they were plentiful, they were also a prized source of food and were eventually hunted to extinction.

The last known sighting of a Dodo bird was more than three

centuries ago by a sailor in **1662.**
So, if you are asking 'Where is
the Dodo Bird?' The simple
answer is that *it's gone forever!*

Fast forward to the spring of
2020. Our city, our nation, our
world is enveloped in the
COVID-19 crisis. Virtually no
city, state or country has been left
untouched by the virus. *It's
literally wrecked devastation on
millions.* Worldwide there have
been almost 3 Million confirmed
cases of the virus. Hundreds of
thousands of people have died
during this pandemic. Economies
have been hit hard,
unemployment is off the charts
and people's lives have been
turned upside down.

Today's question is **NOT** 'Where
is the Dodo Bird' but.............

WHERE IS GOD???

The simple answer is that God is still right here. **He never left.** The Bible says, 'He never leaves or forsakes us.' Well, the natural follow up question is if that's really true, why are we going thru so much pain? The more comprehensive answer is that we are going thru a *wilderness moment.* These are the moments where we meet God up close & personal! These are the moments we connect to God like we've never connected before! These are the moments where our faith is tested to its very limits!

It's important that we remember that the wilderness place as told in the Bible is **never** a place of abandonment. For example, when Hagar ran from the abuse of her mistress Sarai, it's in the wilderness that she met the Lord. And when the Israelites were delivered from slavery in Egypt, it was the wilderness wanderings that tested them and reoriented them towards God. Jesus himself experienced wilderness moments when he was tempted by Satan!

Likewise, for you! COVID-19 is definitely a wilderness moment. It's your chance to grow closer to the Lord. It's your chance to reconnect with the God of the Red Sea. It's your chance to lean into HIM as you've never done before! Let me encourage you with these words from the Book of Isaiah:

Isaiah 40:31 They that **wait** upon the Lord shall renew their strength; they shall mount up with wings as eagles; they shall run, and not be weary; and they shall walk, and not faint.

(In this verse the word **'wait'** means to bind, weave & grow closer to the Lord).

WHERE IS THE DODO BIRD??? GONE FOREVER!!!

WHERE IS GOD??? HE IS RIGHT HERE!!!

**A Rose by any other
name would
smell just as sweet!**

2

God Never Promised You a Rose Garden!

In **1970** country singer **Lynn Anderson** recorded the song: I Never Promised You a Rose Garden. One of the lines in the song says: *'Along with the sunshine, there's gotta be a little rain.'*

Fast forward from 1970 to the Covid-19 pandemic of 2020. As Pastor of SoupMobile Church I've heard lots of complaints over the past several months. Some people are murmuring about how their lives have been turned upside down during this crisis and *they flat out don't like it.* One story I heard early in the pandemic was of a man who was the manager of a local food store. There was lots of panic buying at that time and lines were long at his store. He and his staff were working long hours just to keep the shelves stocked.

When a local TV reporter interviewed him, the store manager spent the entire interview **complaining and whining about his own plight.** Not the plight of his employees, or his customers or the millions of people who lost their jobs because of the pandemic. He complained about the long hours, the antsy customers & the pressure of managing the store.

As Pastor I have heard my fair share of similar stories from people whose lives have been adversely affected by the pandemic. My response is always the same. I do **NOT** make light of the problems they are having. **These problems are real.** What I do say to them is that what really counts are not the problems but how we **respond** to them. After all, God never promised us a rose garden. In fact, the Bible tells us in the book of John that we will have tribulation. *The truth is that everyone has his/her share of unpleasantness & challenging circumstances over the course of a lifetime.* This is simply part of the human experience. It's our **response** to those challenges that defines us.

For example, the Store Manager could have acknowledged the difficulties he was having but **focused on the blessings.** The mere fact that he still had a job while others were losing there's was a blessing.
The fact that he hadn't caught the virus was certainly a blessing!

Beyond that God was giving him the perfect opportunity to bless his fellow man by keeping the store shelves stocked. So instead of whining & complaining *he should have been thanking God for the blessings.*

In life we often do not have a choice about what happens to us. **However, we do have a choice on how we respond.** As the song says, 'Along with the sunshine there's gotta be a little rain.' Right now, with the pandemic it's **raining pretty hard.** Nonetheless you still have a choice on how you will respond. I would gently encourage you to see this pandemic as an **opportunity.** A chance to rise up and bless your fellowman. An opportunity to make the best out of a difficult situation. Remember God says, 'He works out all things together for the good.' This means even bad things, even pandemics. This pandemic is your **opportunity** to bless your fellowman with your own special gifts. It could be as a store manager who keeps the shelves stocked; the person who cuts his elderly neighbor's grass; the guy who helps feed the hungry; the pastor who prays for his flock; the stranger who gives a listening ear or the passerby who gives a friendly smile. Remember...

GOD <u>NEVER</u> PROMISED YOU A ROSE GARDEN, BUT IN THE GARDEN OF LIFE YOU WILL HAVE SUNSHINE & RAIN. HOW YOU RESPOND TO THAT RAIN WILL BE THE <u>DEFINING</u> MOMENT OF YOUR LIFE.

The women's suffrage
movement was a decades
long fight to win the
right to vote for women
in the United States and
was finally achieved in
1920!

3
The Smartest Person in the Room!

Recently I celebrated my **39th Birthday** on **August 18, 2020.** Well, er, ah, um, maybe **39** is just a smidge off, but *that's my story & I'm sticking to it*.

However, I would humbly suggest to you that if we went back in time exactly **100 years** ago to **August 18, 1920,** a far more important event took place. An event which makes my birthday pale in comparison.

On that date one hundred years ago the **19th Amendment** to the U.S. Constitution was ratified

allowing women the right to vote.
NOW LET THAT SINK IN!
Just imagine that there was
actually a time in our nation's history when women were <u>NOT</u> allowed to vote. This is
unimaginable today, but back
then a woman simply could **<u>NOT</u>**
vote!

I remember as a young boy
growing up in Detroit, Michigan
my late father telling me that
sometimes *'The Smartest Person in the Room is a woman.'*
He was teaching me from a very
young age that everyone is
important & everyone has
something to offer. He instilled in
me the belief that we are **all created equal** in God's eyes,
regardless of our sex, race, color,
creed, ethnicity, or cultural
background. Where did my father
learn this valuable lesson? The
Bible! Of the **3,237** people named

in the Bible, **188** of them were women and my oh my, did they *make a huge impact.*

In fact, many of these women were **flat out extraordinary.** There are entire books in the Bible that feature these amazing women! They were indeed some of the 'Smartest People in the Room.'

Beyond the Bible, we could name woman after woman who has blessed our planet. **Hedy Lamar** was not only a famous actress from the 40's, but she also invented a radar guidance system for torpedoes that literally helped us win **World War 2.**

Or how about the **#3** women featured in the **2017 Movie titled: Hidden Figures.** It was a true-life story of three African American women, known as *'human computers,'* who rose thru the ranks of **NASA** & used their incredible math skills to help launch **astronaut John Glenn** into space AND get him home safely.

The bigger lesson here is what my late father taught me many years ago. We are all equal. We may be different in our sex, race, color, creed, origin, or cultural background but we are all equal and we all have something to offer.

So, who is the smartest person in the room--***God's room???*** Sometimes it will be a woman, but it could also be a man, a disabled person, a child or even a person who is totally different from you. They all have something to offer. So, let's reconsider those two key dates in history!

August 18, <u>2020</u>
My 39th—(ish)
Birthday, not
such a Big Deal!
August 18, <u>1920</u>
Women win the
right to vote, a
HUGE DEAL!

The Guinness Book of World Records says the Bible is the best-selling book of all time. The 2nd best-selling book of all time? You guessed it! The Guinness Book of World Records!

4

The Prodigal Nation

By any measure we are living in difficult times. There is no way to sugarcoat the fact that the **COVID-19 pandemic has hit our nation hard.** And while every country on the planet has been impacted, it seems that the United States of America is being especially hard hit.

In the United States alone there have been THREE MILLION Covid-19 cases reported along with a mind blowing & staggering 132,000+ deaths. Unemployment is surpassing 15%. *Many people, families, businesses & churches are just struggling to survive.*

Recently one of my fellow Pastors said to me that *'God is surely punishing America.'* I told him I had another take on what is going on with the pandemic. I'll tell you what I told him. Is it just possible that we have become a **Prodigal Nation?** Is it just possible that God is **NOT** punishing us but that we've simply moved away from God's sphere of protection? Is it just possible that we've brought these problems on ourselves by kicking God right out of our lives?

We all know the story in the Bible of the Prodigal Son. It's about an immature young man whose family was very wealthy. The young man decided that he wanted to receive his family inheritance immediately. This in spite of the fact that his older brother was first in line to inherit and the more obvious fact that his father was still alive & well.

Nonetheless the father granted his request *(God does give us free will)* and gave him his inheritance right on the spot. The young man quickly took the money and left town & went to a foreign land **where he spent the money in riotous living.** He quickly ran out of money & then there was a famine in the land, and he had to take a job feeding pigs.

When the light bulb finally went off in his head that he had goofed up--**BIGTIME,** he then decided to return home to his father. The Bible says in the Book of Luke: *'While he was still a long way off, his father saw him & had compassion; he ran to him, threw his arms around him & kissed him.'* Is it just possible, that much like the **Prodigal Son,** we've left home & become the **Prodigal Nation?** Think about it. Over the past **50+** years we've taken God out of our <u>schools,</u> our <u>businesses,</u> our <u>courts</u> and also out of our <u>public</u> institutions. Incredibly we've even said that the **TEN Commandments** are **<u>not</u>** suitable for public display. What we've done is say to God, **THANKS, BUT NO THANKS!**

Isn't that just what the Prodigal Son said to his father? Thanks, but see you later. I don't need you & I'm off to live life on my own terms. Like it or not, *in many ways we've become the Prodigal Nation over the past 50+ years!*

It's important to note that the father in the Bible story did <u>NOT</u> punish his foolish son. He simply honored the son's wishes. *In truth the son's troubles were self-inflicted.* God is **<u>NOT</u>** punishing

America. HE, like the Prodigal father is simply honoring our wishes to go it on our own. In essence, by kicking God out of our lives over the past **50+ years** we've shot ourselves in the foot & left ourselves open to the enemy. Is there a solution? Is there a chance for redemption? Will God even consider taking us back? These questions are clearly answered in the Bible in the Book of 2 Chronicles:

> *'If my people who are called by my name humble themselves & pray and seek my face and turn from their wicked ways, then I will hear from heaven & will forgive their sin & heal their land.'*

"Faith *is* taking the first step, *even when* you can't see the whole staircase."
Martin Luther King Jr.

5

I Believe!

I Believe in God! I Believe in Angels! I Believe in Prayer!

How about you? What do you believe in??? For many of us the above three statements ring true.

However, it's also a truth that sometimes believing in God, Angels & Prayer is *easier said than done.*
This is understandable! After all we can't see God and it's for sure that Angels can be hard to spot when they are out & about.

Finally praying to God when you can't actually see him in person can sometimes be a little dicey.

What's the common denominator in this whole **'I Believe'** thing??? It's a little *(well actually a BIG)* thing called <u>**FAITH!**</u>

However, there is this funny quirk about faith. Have you noticed that when things are going good in your life that your faith walk seems to be a piece of cake! It's **EASY-PEASY.** However, when times get tough that **Easy-Peasy** faith walk can get a little more uncertain. When I ask my congregation what time in their life did they grow closest to the Lord, they overwhelmingly say it was in the <u>**tough times!**</u> So, what's up with that? Our faith is the most dicey in the tough times but yet we grow closer to God in those very same tough times.

WHY? The answer is that in the good times we don't need to lean into the Lord as much. We can sing his praises, raise up our hands in church & say HE is the *greatest thing since sliced bread.* But because things are going so well, we can afford to be a little lax in our faith walk. However, when times are tough and all seems lost, HE is all we've got. We have to lean into him! We have to trust him! We have to have faith!

So just how *much faith* do you need to be able to believe in God, Angels, & Prayer??? It seems that the answer is:

<u>NOT MUCH!</u>

Yeah, you heard right, we don't need a lot of faith to get results.

Hey, this is pretty good news for all of us low achievers. Jesus himself said you only need faith the size of a **mustard seed** to move mountains.

The mustard seed is one of the smallest seeds on the planet but yet when planted it will grow up to 12ft tall. *And whalla, us low achievers become high achievers!* In my own lifetime I've seen a lot. Good times & not so good times. But I've never seen anything like the current **COVID-19** pandemic we are going thru. I'm guessing neither have you! There is no way to sugarcoat the fact that these are some tough times. These are the times when our faith can get a little shaky but also the times, we can grow closer to the Lord. These are the times when our faith can & will move mountains!

Preachers all over the world are urging their congregations to have great faith. Might I humbly point you in the **opposite** direction. As the Pastor of SoupMobile Church I want to take the pressure **off** of you. Yes, you heard right, let's get that pressure off of you! All I'm asking is that you have just a ***little bit of faith***. Just the ***tiniest bit.*** Just a ***smidge of faith!*** In fact, all I'm asking for is no bigger faith than the size of the mustard seed.

Remember Jesus himself said that tiny faith is all you need. And with that little faith you can and will believe in ***God, Angels & Prayer!***

p.s. THERE IS ONE OTHER THING I BELIEVE IN--- MIRACLES!

-

Oh boy, Apple Pie!

6

Don't Eat the Pie!

There was a workman who worked hard every day. Most days were good ones for him but on one particular day his job was more **difficult than normal.** It seemed everything that could go wrong did go wrong.

At the end of the day, he was hot, tired, and hungry. He decided to stop at a local diner before heading home. At the diner he told the waitress he wanted a <u>cup of coffee,</u> a <u>piece of pie</u> and *a few kind words.*

The waitress promptly brought his coffee & pie and started to walk away. The workman called her back and said "Hey, where are the *kind words?"* The waitress came back, leaned over, smiled, and whispered,

"Don't Eat the Pie."

How about you??? Do you need to hear some kind words? Truth be told, we all need to hear some kind words sometimes.

When you think about it, our lives are made up of good days and then sometimes <u>not</u> so good days. In fact, the Bible tells us in the Book of John that **'We will have tribulation.'** The good news is that it's <u>not</u> tribulation all the time but nonetheless troubles, hardships & difficulties can be part of our life journey.

With the **Covid-19 pandemic** lingering on, it seems that we are going thru one of those times of tribulation. Much like the workman, some of our days have been particularly difficult. We all need some of that proverbial hot cup of coffee, a piece of pie AND a few *kind words!*

As Pastor of SoupMobile Church I am in the business of giving out kind words.

However, it's also my business <u>not</u> to sugarcoat the tough times!

There is no getting around the impact the Covid-19 pandemic has had on our City, our Nation & the World. Worldwide there have been more than 30 Million cases & over 1 Million deaths. In the United States alone we've had almost 7 Million cases & 200,000 deaths.

This is certainly a time when we all need some kind words! So here goes!

Kind Word No#1: We

are going thru the fire, but the fire is <u>NOT</u> our final destination. We will get thru to the other side!

Kind Word No#2: God

has NOT forgotten about you! He promises you that HE will never leave or forsake you!

Kind Word No#3: Jesus

went to the Cross for you! Make no mistake about it; HE is still here for you!

Notice that I am <u>not</u> asking you to have a **Pollyanna** view of what's happening with Covid-19. However, I am asking you to <u>NOT</u> to eat the pie of negativity.

Remember the Bible is full of stories of trials & then victory. Can you say Red Sea! The Israelites were trapped at the edge of the Red Sea with Pharaoh

& his army bearing down. Yes, for the Israelites those were hard times! Talk about despair! Talk about needing kind words!

Back then things looked hopeless for God's people--just like they do now with **Covid-19.**

But guess what? Just *when things looked there darkest*, God stepped in & parted the Red Sea.

He will do the same for you. As a Pastor I want to remind you that the Lord is still on the throne, and he will fight for you. *You will get across your Red Sea!* Just remember what the waitress said to the workman:

DON'T EAT THE PIE--of negativity!

Real friends pray together!

7
I Prayed, So What's Taking So Long?

From a very young age we are taught to pray. One popular children's prayer is a classic from the 18th century--'Now I Lay Me Down to Sleep.' However, have you noticed that as we get older sometimes our prayer lives **hit a snag.**

We pray for stuff and sometimes it seems that nothing is happening. Yet the Bible tells us in no uncertain terms that prayer does work. For example:
1 John 5:14: If we ask anything according to his will, he hears us.
James 5:16: The fervent prayer of a righteous man availeth much.

John 16:24: Ask & ye shall receive, that your joy may be full.

All of these verses seem to clearly be saying that if you pray to God, *you will get results!* Yet many times we pray and seemingly nothing happens! So, what's up with that??? Does God really hear our prayers? Do prayers only work once in a while? Is it possible that prayers never work? **What's going on with this prayer thing???** <u>**The answer is twofold!**</u>

First, we need to realize that sometimes God will say **NO** to our prayers. I remember as a child growing up in Detroit, Michigan (the car Capital of the world) that at the **age of 10** I asked my mother if I could drive the car. **SHE SAID NO!** I begged, pleaded, and even threw a minor temper tantrum. Her answer was still **NO.** She said no because she knew I wasn't old enough, mature enough or big enough to drive. She knew if she said yes & let me drive, *that disaster was just around the corner.* And while I didn't understand her NO at the time, I do now, and I am eternally grateful to my mother for saying no. She saved us both a lot of grief.

Likewise, God will sometimes say **NO** to your prayers *because you aren't ready or mature enough for a yes.* As a Pastor I often tell my congregation that a NO from God can be a very good thing. And while you may not understand the no at the time, just know that God *(just like my mother)* is always working in your best interests.

The second part of the answer to whether prayers are effective is the knowing that when God says YES, *sometimes you don't see the results right away.* And because you can't see immediate results you might think your prayers have gone unanswered.

In the Bible this happened to Abraham. When God told him to sacrifice his son Isaac up on the mountain, Abraham was believing & praying that God would provide a substitute sacrifice so he would not have to slay his only son Isaac. Yet on the barren mountain there was no other acceptable sacrifice to be found. Little did Abraham know that God was sending a 'Ram' up the *other side of the mountain* that was to be used for the sacrifice.

This is how it works with us sometimes. God hears your prayer & sends the answer (like the Ram) but we think he's forgotten about us or has ignored our prayer because we can't see the answer that's coming up on the **other side of our mountain.** So, what's the bottom line on this prayer thing? Does God hear our prayers? Does he answer them? The answer is that he **absolutely hears & absolutely answers** our prayers. He only asks that you...Trust his timing & trust his answer...

EVEN IF THAT ANSWER HAPPENS TO BE A <u>NO!</u>

Can you hear me now???

8

Number #1

In **1877** Rutherford B. Hayes was elected as the **19**th President of the United States. He was a highly educated man who went to Harvard Law School. His wife Lucy was the first **1st Lady** to have a college degree. They were both strong advocates for civil rights & Lucy was a staunch supporter for women getting the right to vote. By all accounts they were good people and Hayes served well as President. However, for historians Hayes is often best remembered as being the President that had the **1**st **telephone** installed in the White House.

Can you guess what the telephone number was for that first telephone in the White House? If you guessed number '1', you would be absolutely correct. As it should be! After all the White House is certainly one of the most important institutions in our country & it was the first phone installed there, so the telephone **Number #1** was most appropriate.

But that was **1877.** Let's *fast forward to 2020.* Who or what is Number #1 in your life? Most people would quickly say the Lord is number one in their lives, but I wonder if we say this too quickly & casually. It's true that times were simpler back in **1877.** While they did have the telephone, there were no cars, computers, video games, social media, or cell phones. In many ways it was easier to connect with God back then & make him Number #1.

Nowadays in our fast paced, hectic, social media world, we can easily get distracted from connecting with God.

What happens when we don't make God Number #1 in our lives? The simple answer is **'NOT SO GOOD THINGS CAN HAPPEN.'** Can you say Prodigal Son? When he left the safety & security of his Father's home bad things happened almost immediately. The Bible says he put *riotous living number #1 in his life* and in short order he lost everything and became penniless.

Note that God **(the Father)** did not cause the son to become penniless & destitute. All of his troubles were self-inflicted.

Likewise, for us! When we don't make God Number #1, bad things can happen but it's not God who is doing it. Most of the time we are doing it to ourselves, and our woes are indeed self-afflicted.

So, while most people would quickly say that God is Number #1 in their lives, actions speak louder than words. I would ask you this simple question. Are you looking to the

Lord **'EVERY-DAY'** for his help & guidance? The key word here is **EVERY-DAY.** Are you making a connection with God every single day of your life? Or do you get distracted by all of the bells, whistles and glitter of our fast-paced world?

I 'get it' that we are living in busy times and there is a lot of competition for our attention. Nonetheless I would encourage you to spend some time with the Lord every day. It doesn't have to be every minute of the day, but he is certainly well worth some of your time.

How about starting with a simple *'Good Morning God'* when you wake up. How about *thanking* him throughout the day for whatever good is happening in your life.

You can *talk* with God just like he is your best friend, because guess what—HE is your best friend!

TIME'S WERE SIMPLER BACK IN 1877 BUT PUTTING GOD 1ST IN OUR LIVES IS NO LESS IMPORTANT TODAY!

"Those who can't change their minds, can't change anything." George Bernard Shaw

9

It's Crazy!

I have a good friend who was looking at his social media feed the other day and he said-- **It's Crazy!** He had been reading a story about how deeply divided our country is. It's true, we are divided on everything from politics, race, creed, color, gender, religious beliefs and so much more. But here's the real problem. *This divisiveness has gone beyond just a simple difference of opinion.*

Our country is currently experiencing a spike in violence, anger, name calling, foul language, false accusations & just plain old hatred.

There doesn't seem to be too much civility anymore.

My late father used to say that *'Reasonable people can reasonably disagree.'* This made sense to me as a child, and it makes sense to me today. My father taught me that just because a person has a different opinion that didn't mean you can't be civil to that person. He taught me that it's okay to disagree with someone but to *do it with grace.*

Sadly, there don't seem to be any reasonable disagreements anymore. We are polarized as a nation, with each side digging in and defending their turf with name calling, shouting, anger and violence. As my friend said, **It's Crazy!**

Some would say that this wrongful behavior is no big deal. However, I would contend that what we are really doing is spitting in the face of Jesus. Strong words--I know, but remember it was Jesus himself who said that the two greatest commandments were to *'Love the Lord thy God with all thy heart AND to love thy neighbor as thyself.'*

I promise you; we are NOT loving our neighbor as ourselves. Jesus was the master at *reasonably disagreeing* with people. When the crowd wanted to stone the woman caught in adultery, he could have unloaded on them with hate, anger, bitterness & harsh words. Instead, he reasonably disagreed by saying, *'He who has never sinned cast the first stone.'*

Some people blame politics on what's caused our county to be so divided, but that's just a cop out. In truth we've been spitting in God's face for years. Over the past 50 years we've taken God out of our schools, our businesses, our courts, and our public institutions. We've even said that the **10 Commandments** are not suitable for public display.

No, we can't blame our bad behavior on politics. This is about drifting away from the Lord and the farther we drift the more atrocious our behavior becomes.

What's the solution to this crazy behavior? It's two simple words: **Stop it!** Yes, just stop it. **Stop** the trash talk, **stop** the foul language, **stop** the violence—**just stop it.**

It's okay to have strong beliefs; it's okay to take a stand; it's okay to express your opinion. What's not okay is spitting in the face of Jesus with our abominable & sinful behavior.

It's just crazy!!! Just stop it!!! Stop it now!!!

Let's all follow the example that Jesus set. Let's start loving our neighbor as ourselves and do it regardless of their belief system, their race, color, creed, or political persuasion.

Let's get some Jesus type civility back in our nation before it's too late!

Let's stop the name calling, the foul language, the bitterness, and the violence. Let's replace it with a healthy dose of Love, Caring & Compassion.

I miss my late father. He was from a different generation, but I learned so much from him. He would readily admit that he was far from perfect, but he did have a certain kindness & grace about him.

And when he did disagree with someone, he did it with kindness & understanding.

And I know in my heart of hearts that he was right all along...

REASONABLE PEOPLE CAN REASONABLY DISAGREE

& that's <u>NOT</u> Crazy!!!

Whatever God has called you to do, he wants you to do it well.

10
TRASH MAN

Tragically, Martin Luther King was assassinated on April 4, 1968. What most people don't know is that he was only **39 years old.** Nonetheless he left a powerful legacy. One of my favorite MLK quote's is:

"If a man is called to be a street sweeper, he should sweep streets even as a Michelangelo painted, or Beethoven composed music or Shakespeare wrote poetry. He should sweep streets so well that all the hosts of heaven and earth will pause to say, here lived a great street sweeper who did his job well."

As Pastor of SoupMobile Church one of the most common questions I am asked is **'What's my purpose in life?'** In other words, why was I even born? What does God want me to do with my life?

For some of us he wants us to be Street-Sweepers! But not just ordinary Street-Sweepers but <u>masterful ones</u> like Martin Luther King spoke of. Others are born to be athletes, CEO's of large corporations, homemakers, painters, artists, teachers, authors, & a few are called to be a Trash-Man.

I'll come back to that Trash-Man thing a little later in this sermon. The bottom line is that whatever God has called you to do, he wants you to do it well. The Bible addresses this in the book of Colossians where it says, *'Whatsoever you do, do it with excellence, as to the LORD.'* It's important to understand that we all have a purpose. God has a divine plan for your life. Sometimes we struggle to recognize & understand what that plan is, but nonetheless it's still there for us to fulfill. In the book titled **Clowns of God by Morris West,** there's a story of Christ returning to earth for a brief visit at a school for children with Down Syndrome. In this fictional story, Jesus picks up a little girl & says, *"I know what you all are thinking, why don't I just* *heal her. Well, I could do it, but I won't. I gave this little one a gift that none of you has—it's eternal innocence. To you she looks imperfect, but to me she is flawless. She is necessary for you. She will evoke the kindness in you that brings out your humanity. Her infirmity will prompt you to have gratitude for your own good fortune. This little one is my sign to you, treasure her."*

What this story is saying is that we all have a purpose in life, even someone with **Down Syndrome!**

At the SoupMobile we have our own *life purpose,* which is feeding the homeless & needy children in Dallas, Texas. We've been doing that mission since our founding in 2003. We are laser like focused on paying forward the gift of the Cross and we believe we best serve Christ by serving the ones he calls the 'least of these.'

However, since the COVID-19 pandemic began we've been operating with a skeleton crew of **#5** people. All five bring their own special talents to the table. Ms. Judy is our

Energizer Bunny who wears multiple hats; Mike is our 'Jack of all Trades' guy who can fix pretty much anything; Chef Stanley is our Chef extraordinaire; Jerald is our Tech whiz & I'm the Trash-Man.

Now I can see you scratching your heads and saying but aren't you the Pastor & Executive Director of the SoupMobile? What's the deal with you being a Trash-Man? What's up with that?

Well yes, I am the Pastor & Executive Director, but every day, I faithfully haul our trash out to the dumpster.

And much like Martin Luther King's street-sweeper, I strive to do my trash job with excellence & a real sense of pride.

I believe I have multiple purposes in life but clearly being a Trash-Man is one of them. You too have a purpose in life. Find that purpose, fulfill that purpose & do it with excellence!

NEVER DOUBT THAT YOU HAVE A PURPOSE IN LIFE, EVEN IF IT'S TO BE A TRASH-MAN!

I will sustain you and I will rescue you! The Book of Isaiah 46:4

11

Rescue Me

Back in **1965** Ms. Fontana Bass recorded the **No.#1 hit single titled Rescue Me!** Here's a few of the lyrics from that song:

Rescue me & take me in your arms. Come on & take my heart, take your love & conquer every part. Cause I'm lonely and I'm blue, I need you & your love too!

This song is typical of the early 60's songwriting that spoke about love & sometimes heartbreak. Fast forward from the early 60's to the **pandemic of 2020** and I think you will find that the words of this song are still relevant today. Especially that part about feeling lonely & blue.

We're all getting battered by the **Covid-19 virus.** There is no getting around the negative impact that the pandemic has had on our City, our Nation & the World.

Worldwide there have been almost 50 Million cases & more than 1 Million deaths. In the United States alone we've had over 9 Million cases & 230,000 deaths.

Unemployment is hitting new highs; mental health issues are on the rise & many people are feeling isolated & alone. We're all wondering when this misery will end.

And much like the **'Rescue Me' song by Ms. Fontana Bass, we're** all feeling just a little *'lonely & blue.'* But just know, we are in good company.

Throughout Bible history, God's children have experienced adversity & had their own version of feeling 'lonely & blue' & needing to be rescued.

Remember the story of the **Israelites trapped at the edge of the Red Sea** with Pharaoh and his army bearing down?

Oh yes, the Israelites were feeling **lonely and blue.** Nonetheless God heard their cries and saved them by parting the Red Sea.

Or how about **Daniel & the Lion's Den!** That had to be a little bit dicey for Daniel—don't you think? But once again God stepped in and sent an Angel to keep the mouths of the Lions closed.

And then there's **David & Goliath.** Here's a little teenage shepherd boy going up against the biggest, baddest dude on the planet. The Bible says that God was with David! And sure, enough David won that battle!

Note that in all of these stories, God's people experienced adversity, just as we are today with Covid-19. God doesn't promise that your life will be all roses and honey, but he does promise that he will,

'Never leave or forsake you.'

He didn't forsake Moses & the Israelites at the Red Sea; he didn't forget about Daniel in the Lion's Den; and he was with David as he fought the giant Goliath.

Likewise, he hasn't forgotten you. He knows you are *'lonely & blue.'* He knows if you need to be rescued.

However, remember it's a two-way street with God. While he will do all the heavy lifting, you need to do your own part. You need to take an active part in your own rescue!

Think of it as a partnership---with God as the senior partner & you as the junior partner. In the book of Psalms it says, "I will save those who love me & I will protect those who acknowledge me as Lord. When they call to me, I will answer them & I will rescue them."

Regretfully, in many ways we've drifted away from God in the last 50 years. We've taken him out of our schools, our businesses & our courts.

Regretfully & sadly, we've even said the **Ten Commandments** are not suitable for public display!

Much like the Prodigal son, we need to head back home into the loving & warm embrace of the Father.

And when you get there, if you are wondering what to say to God, just repeat the words from that 1965 Rescue Me hit song by Ms. Fontana Bass...

Rescue me and take me in your arms, come & take my heart, take your Love & conquer every part. Cause I'm lonely & blue, I need you and your love too!

-

The Mustard Seed is one of the smallest seeds on the Planet, but when planted, can grow to more than 12ft tall.

12

The Mustard Seed

2020 will go down as one of the most difficult years in the history of the United States of America. I'm talking about the **Covid-19** pandemic.

The worst pandemic in more than **100 years.** There is no **sugarcoating** the devastation it's caused. There have been more than 50 Million cases worldwide with more than 1 Million deaths. In the United States there have been more than 10 Million cases and 250,000 deaths.

In our home state of Texas, there have been more than 1 million confirmed cases. It's not an exaggeration to say that Covid-19 may be the most difficult crisis we will ever face in our lifetime.

Recently one of my parishioners came to me and said that she felt like she had *Covid-19 fatigue.* I told her that was perfectly understandable. She went on to say that she also felt like she had *'faith fatigue.'*

I asked her to explain. She said that when the pandemic began, her faith was strong & she believed with all her heart that everything would be okay. However, as the pandemic lingered on, she felt like her faith walk was weakening. It was getting harder and harder for her to trust and to have faith that God would get her & her family thru this ordeal.

How about you? Are you having **Covid-19 fatigue?** Are you having your own version of faith fatigue?

If you are, let me tell you what I told my parishioner. First, I told her, welcome to the human race. I went on to say that it's okay if your faith isn't 100%; it's okay if you don't have Billy Graham type faith and it's okay to doubt.

It's important that we all understand that doubt is **NOT** an abandonment of our faith. Doubt is actually a part of your faith walk.

So, if you are having doubts, I say again-- welcome to the human race. And just how does God feel about doubters? Well in the book of Jude it says: *'Be merciful to those who doubt.'* So, if this Covid-19 pandemic is giving you **'faith fatigue'** just know that God still loves you just the same.

Now you may be saying, well thanks for the encouragement Pastor but you still haven't addressed the fact that my faith is weak.

Well, here's what I've got to say about your weak faith. *Well done! Nice going! You're doing great! Keep up the good work!*

You ask, how can I possibly congratulate you for your weak faith. Well guess what?

God knew that **99%** of us would **not** have Billy Graham type faith. He knew we would sometimes struggle in our faith walk. And God, in his infinite Grace & mercy gave us an out. He said that not only is it okay to have weak faith, *it's also good enough.*

Let's check out what Jesus himself said about this faith thing. In the book of Matthew, Jesus said that if you have faith as small as a **Mustard Seed** you can move mountains.

Now let's put that into context. The Mustard seed is one of the smallest seeds on the planet. In a typical small sized seed packet, there are more than **5,000 mustard seeds.** That's how tiny they are!

Jesus was telling us two things here. One, it's absolutely okay to have faith fatigue & two, as long as you have even the smallest amount of faith, **(even as small as a mustard seed),** you will get thru this Covid-19 pandemic.

I know it looks like this pandemic will never end. I know many of you are hurting. I know some of you are having Covid-19 fatigue.

I also know that many of you are having **faith** fatigue. I want you to know it's all okay!

Just remember that even if your faith is as small as a mustard seed...

God will honor that faith & he will move <u>your</u> mountain, whatever it is!

Bette Davis in All About Eve (1950)

13
Fasten Your Seatbelts

In the classic 1950 film titled: **All About Eve,** the esteemed actress Bette Davis uttered one of the most infamous movie lines of all time. She said, *'Fasten your seatbelts, it's going to be a bumpy night.'*

In many ways our nation seems to be experiencing our own version of a **bumpy night.** In many cities crime is on the increase, poverty rates are climbing, peaceful protests often turn into rioting and violence, mental health issues are skyrocketing, drug use is off the charts, weather related problems are on the rise & it seems like all of California is on fire. And as a nation we seem to be experiencing too much hate, too much anger & too much divisiveness.

And on top of everything else we are in the **midst of the worst pandemic in over 100 years.** Covid-19 is literally wreaking havoc on our nation & the entire world. Indeed, as Bette Davis said, we need to fasten our seatbelts as *we are facing bumpy night after bumpy night.*

The real question many are asking, is just how do we respond to all of these bumpy nights? I would encourage you to look at these bumpy nights as an opportunity—*Yes, as a unique & extraordinary opportunity!!!*

Now I can see you scratching your head & saying, well gee whiz Pastor, the world is falling apart—my own life is awfully bumpy right now & you want me to see these bumpy nights as an **opportunity?** Well—yes, I do! Let me explain!

In the Bible Jesus says that the two greatest commandments are to '*Love the Lord thy God with all thy heart and to Love your neighbor as yourself.*'

That 1st commandment to love God seems to be the easier one. It's the loving your neighbor as yourself where we seem to have the most trouble. It's no secret that we live in a divisive world. But maybe, *just maybe we can use these bumpy nights as the stimulus to start making a real difference in this world.* Maybe we can use these bumpy nights to motivate us to reach out to our fellowman in **Love, Caring & Compassion.**

And remember, there is a payoff for you when you bless others. In the book of Proverbs, it says: *'Whoever brings blessings will be enriched & one who waters will himself be watered.'* In other words, when you bless others, God makes it a point to bless you!

So now you may be saying, okay Pastor, I hear you about using these hard times as the springboard to help others but remember Pastor my nights are awfully bumpy right now. Any suggestions on just how I can bless my fellowman in the midst of all this chaos?

Well yes, I do have a few suggestions. Let me start by telling you that sometimes **the littlest things can make the biggest difference.** For example, how about giving someone a kind word or a friendly greeting, maybe a smile, a pat on the back, maybe buy a burger for a homeless person, put a quarter in someone's parking meter so they don't get a ticket, or how about baking some cookies for someone.

Even better, how about **praying** for your fellowman? We can all do that no matter how bumpy our nights are!

Yes, just as Bette Davis said, we are all going thru some bumpy nights right now. However, I would encourage you to look at these bumpy nights as your opportunity to pay forward the gift of the Cross by blessing your fellowman.

I leave you with these words from one of the smartest people that ever walked this planet—His name--Albert Einstein, he said:

"Only a Life lived for others is a Life worthwhile."

(See next page for Author's note)

(Authors Note)
These words by
Albert Einstein
have served as the
SoupMobile's
'Motto' since our
founding in 2003!

An Empty Tomb???

14

Three Simple Words!

In a recent Peanuts Comic Strip there was a picture of good old lovable Charlie Brown, and he is on the phone with God. He says,

Hello God, we need your help down here. The world has gone mad. Please hear and answer our prayers!
Thank you & Amen!

Well Charlie Brown may have said it *but we're all thinking it.* In many ways it seems like the world has gone mad. We are indeed living in difficult times. In many cities crime is on the increase; poverty rates are climbing; peaceful protests often turn into rioting and violence;

mental health issues are skyrocketing, drug use is off the charts, weather problems are on the rise with a record number of hurricanes hitting the Southern coast of the United States AND it seems like all of California is on fire as they experience their worst wildfire season ever!

Add to all of the above is the **incredible political divide** in our country. Any sense of decency, honor and goodwill seems to have gone by the wayside. Each side has dug in and its **Attack! Attack! & Attack some more!**

And on top of everything else we are in **the midst of the worst pandemic in over 100 years,** with Covid-19 wreaking havoc on our nation & our world. Charlie Brown was right--'The world has gone mad.' So, what's the solution? Is all lost? Is there any hope at all? Well yes, there is hope & it comes from above. That hope consists of Three Simple Words, **HE is Risen!** Now normally we hear this phrase **every Easter** when we celebrate the resurrection of Jesus.

But oh my gosh, do we need to hear it now--**HE is Risen!** But let's put this into context by looking at it from another angle. What's it mean if Christ isn't risen, if he wasn't resurrected on the **3rd day???**

In the Book of Corinthians, the Apostle Paul says: *'If Christ has not been raised, then all our preaching is useless, **and your faith is in vain.**'*

What the Bible is telling us is that Christ is our way out of this mess. In the book of John, Jesus himself says *'I am the Way, the Truth and the Life.'* HE's our way out!

Yeah, just like Charlie Brown said, the world has gone mad. The good news is that **HE is Risen.** And that's where our hope, our salvation and our victory is—in HIM!

There is no sugarcoating the fact that we are going thru difficult times. I'm not asking you to pretend that everything is hunky dory—it's NOT! We 'ARE' going thru the fire and it's incredibly hot! But remember the fire is <u>**NOT**</u> **your final destination.** Yes, we are going 'thru' the fire, but we will come thru to the other side.

Much like the Israelites passing thru the Red Sea! We can only imagine the fear & angst that Moses & his people felt as they were crossing thru the Red Sea. In many ways they must have felt as if their own world had gone mad. But nonetheless they came thru the Red Sea to the safety of the other side.

What I'm asking you to do now is exactly what Charlie Brown did. Put in your own call to God. The phone lines are open. No call waiting, no busy signal & he won't put you on hold. Tell God you need help, just like Charlie Brown did. He will answer your call because of those #3 simple words: **HE is Risen!** Don't wait for next Easter, time is tight—call him now!!! He is waiting for your call....

Psalm 50:15
Call upon me in the day of trouble and I will *deliver* you.

Jeremiah 33:3
Call upon me and I will *answer* you.

Mary Walker, truly one of the most amazing people to ever walk the Planet!!!

15
Dream Big Baby!

Today I'm going to tell you about a very special person. Her name is **Mary Walker,** and she is nothing short of amazing. She was born in Union Springs, Ala. in 1848 & she died in 1969. Let me say it again: **Born in 1848. Died in 1969.** Now I can see some of you doing some quick math in your head and if you came up with the fact that she lived to age **121** you would be absolutely correct.

And as incredible as it was for Mary Walker to live to the **age of 121,** that was **not** the most amazing thing about her. You see Mary dreamed big but before I tell you about her big dreams, let me give you her backstory.

When she was born in **1848,** she was born into slavery. She was the daughter of slave parents who worked on a plantation. At the age of **15** she became a free person when the **Emancipation Proclamation was signed by Abraham Lincoln.** Of course, we all know that while the Emancipation Proclamation technically freed the slaves that the reality was far different. Mary went on to endure more than a century of discrimination. She married at age 20 & had three children. *She eventually outlived her husband & all three of her children.*

Over the years she had many jobs including cooking, cleaning and babysitting. However, she was unable to find any high paying jobs because of the fact that she was a <u>former slave</u>, a <u>female,</u> a <u>person of color</u> & most limiting was the fact that she could <u>not read or write</u>.

When she was born in **1848** it was actually ***illegal*** for a slave to learn to read or write. This is absolutely unimaginable today, but back then it was the law. But Mary dreamed big & believed that with God all things are possible. At the age of **116** she enrolled in night school where in a year's time she learned to read, write, add and subtract.

She was certified by the United States Dept of Education as *the nation's oldest student.* She was recognized by two U.S. Presidents and even took her 1st airplane ride in 1966 at the age of **118** years old. Indeed, Mary Walker dreamed big!

The Bible gives us ample precedent for dreaming big. **Moses** dreamed of freeing the Israelites from the Egyptians. **Joshua** dreamed of conquering the promised land. **David** dreamed of defeating Goliath. And with God on their side all of those dreams came true! **How about you?** Do you have big dreams? Is there something you want to accomplish in your life, but much like Mary Walker you have some big obstacles in the way.

Perhaps you think you are too old or perhaps not educated enough. Maybe this Covid-19 pandemic has you on the defensive. *Maybe you just don't think your big dreams are possible.* Here's what I would say to you about that. On your own your dreams are NOT possible but if you will bring God into the picture, amazing things can AND will happen. The Bible says in the book of Philippians *'You can do all things thru Christ.'* That's what Mary Walker did. With much determination and her strong belief in the Lord she persevered and at the age of **116** began the oldest student who ever went to school in the United States and at that advanced age she did learn to read & write. The key for you to achieve your dreams is to get the right partner. I would encourage you to hook up to an experienced Senior Partner— yes, I'm talking about God. Tap into **HIS** power, **HIS** might, **HIS** ability to get things done. The Bible says that God is *'Able to do exceedingly abundantly more than you could ask or even think to ask.'* Or as I like to say:

DREAM BIG BABY!

Christmas, a special time to celebrate the birth of baby Jesus!

16

All I Want for Christmas!

In **1990** at the age of **22,** Mariah Carey exploded onto the music scene. She was a hit from the get-go, and she has gone on to be one of the most popular and enduring singers of all time. Over the years she has sold more than **200 million records.**

However, it's one particular song that she sang that we want to talk about today. In 1994 Mariah Carey recorded and sang the Christmas song titled:

All I Want for Christmas!

It was incredibly popular in 1994 and even more so today. It's become a Christmas standard & is loved by both children and adults. And as good as the music is and as good as her vocals are in this song, it's the actual words that seem to ring true for us in 2020, which will forever be known as the year of the Covid-19 pandemic.

Here are a few of the words from her 1994 song 'All I want for Christmas.' She sings:

I don't want a lot for Christmas; there is just one thing I need. I don't care about presents underneath the Christmas tree. I just want you for my own, more than you could ever know, make my wish come true!

In the song when Mariah says: I just want 'you' for my own, she is referring to a loved one. However, I would suggest that in this pandemic year of 2020 the **'you'** in our own song of hearts should be for a guy from 2,000 years ago—yes Jesus. And I don't mean this in a religious way. I mean in a very practical life-saving & life-giving way.

In John 6:35 **Jesus** says, *'I am the bread of life; whoever comes to me* **shall not hunger** *and whoever believes in me* **shall never thirst.***'* In this verse the bread of life is not physical bread, but it is the bread of spiritual renewal that can only be found in Jesus Christ.

Let's be honest with ourselves. If ever we needed some spiritual renewal, it's now, this Christmas as we are in the *midst of the worst pandemic in more than 100 years.*

One of my parishioners said that **2020** was the most difficult year of her life. She lost her job, she lost a loved one, her own health declined, & this was **before** the pandemic fully hit. She also said that 2020 was the year she grew <u>closest</u> to the Lord. *This is extraordinary!* The worst year of her life and yet the year she grew <u>closest</u> to the Lord.

However, that shouldn't really be a surprise to any of us. Think about it. When times are good, we can raise our hands and praise the Lord like he's the greatest thing since **sliced bread—and he is!** But in the good times we really don't have to press into him as much. However, when times are bad **(like this pandemic)** he's all we've got. We have to press into him because he's the only viable game in town.

How about you. Do you need some spiritual renewal? Do you need some uplifting? Do you need Jesus? With this pandemic raging many people are answering these three questions **<u>YES-YES & YES!</u>** We want spiritual renewal; we want to be uplifted & we want Jesus!

So now the question becomes, how we do it. How do we get Jesus back in our lives???

Well, the **Bible** tells us exactly what to do in the book of Psalms. It says, 'Call on me and I will answer you.' Yes, it's that simple. *Give God a call.* The phone lines are open. No call waiting, no busy signal & he won't put you on hold.

Yes, back in 1994 Mariah Carey sang the words: 'I don't want a lot for Christmas, there is just one thing I need. I don't care about presents underneath the Christmas Tree, *I just want you for **my** own.'*

As the pastor of SoupMobile Church, I'll take the liberty of changing the <u>last line</u> of the song to:

Jesus, we just want you for <u>our</u> own!!!

Has anyone ever jumped off the Golden Gate Bridge and actually survived???

17

Jumpers

In **1937** they built the **Golden Gate Bridge** in San Francisco, California. When it was built it set a record as the longest & tallest suspension bridge in the entire world. In **1937** they called it one of the *'Wonders of the Modern World.'* The bridge was a huge blessing to the local community and helped with traffic flow and ease of travel, but it also had a dark side. Since the bridge was built in 1937 more than **1,700** people have tried to commit suicide by jumping off the bridge. *Sadly, most of them have been successful.* Only *25 jumpers out of 1,700* have managed to survive the fall. Yes, that's right! **ONLY #25 out of 1,700 jumpers** have survived the fall from the bridge! Those aren't very good odds. However, one man who did beat the odds was Kevin Hines. A few years ago, he was suffering from depression and thought he would end it all by jumping off the **Golden Gate Bridge.** As he pushed off the rail into the night air, he suddenly realized that he did **NOT** want to die. As he fell towards the water below, he cried out to God and said: "What have I done, I don't want to die, Oh God please save me." Yes, Kevin changed his mind about committing suicide **AFTER** he jumped. Even for God, his survival was going to take a big-time miracle. But the good news is that our God is still a God of miracles!

The Lord heard his prayer, but Kevin still hit the water at an incredibly high speed. As a severely injured Kevin was sinking below the water to a certain drowning death, a **Sea Lion** came along and kept pushing Kevin up to the surface to give the Coast Guard time to get to him. Wow, God sent a Sea Lion! Can you say Jonah & the Whale! *There are two key points to Kevin's story:*

1. <u>**GOD IS A GOD OF MIRACLES:**</u> The same God that parted the Red Sea, sent a whale to save Jonah from drowning & knocked down the Walls of Jericho is still alive & well & sent a Sea Lion to save Kevin.

2. <u>**GOD HAS A DIVINE DESTINY FOR YOUR LIFE:**</u> Kevin Hines survived a fall that scientists say is virtually the same as slamming into a brick wall at <u>**75 + miles per hour!**</u> Why did Kevin survive? Because God still had a plan for his life. After Kevin healed up from his injuries, he devoted his life to

helping others who were dealing with suicidal thoughts. Over the years he's spoken to numerous groups all over the country and he has also counseled many individuals on a one-on-one basis. All in all, Kevin Hines is doing well and is personally responsible for saving many lives. God sent a **Sea Lion** to save Kevin because he still had a Divine purpose for his life. *How about you? Do you have a Divine Destiny ahead of you?*

The great **Pastor T.D. Jakes** says that the reason that he knows you still have a Divine Destiny ahead of you is because God woke you up this morning. So, if you are reading this sermon, it means God woke you up today and you still have a Divine Destiny ahead of you. You may be asking what might that Divine Destiny be? I can't say for sure what yours is, but this much I do know. Your Divine Destiny is connected *in some way with blessing your fellowman*. It may not be finding the cure for cancer or fixing global warming. However, whatever God has in store for you will in some way revolve around blessing others! It will be something much like the example of service that Jesus set for us 2,000 years ago. Albert Einstein said, *"Only a Life Lived for Others is a Life Worthwhile."* Jesus said, *"Love your neighbor as yourself."* Much like Kevin Hines, God will save you so that you can achieve your own Devine Destiny!

SO, IF YOU ARE THINKING ABOUT JUMPING, PLEASE DON'T! HOWEVER, IF YOU DO, DON'T BE SURPRISED IF GOD SENDS A SEA LION TO SAVE YOU!!!

**Are you feeling just a little
Shipwrecked???**

18
Shipwrecked!

The late **Billy Graham** tells the story of a man who was shipwrecked and ended up stranded all alone on a deserted island. It was an isolated area and the man had absolutely no hope that he would ever be rescued. Over time he built himself a hut and stocked it with a few of the items that had washed up on shore. The hut kept him dry in the rain and cool in the summer heat. The hut was really all he had of value, and *it was literally his lifeline to sanity.*

One day he was on the other side of the island hunting for food and looked back to see that his hut *was on fire.* He ran back as quickly as he could but by the time he got there everything he had perished in the flames. In just a few moments he lost everything. He cried out to God in anguish. *How could HE let this happen?* His life was already bad enough as he was shipwrecked on this deserted island and now it got even worse as the fire consumed every earthly thing he had.

So, what about you??? *Are you feeling a little shipwrecked?* With the Covid-19 pandemic many people would say they are absolutely feeling shipwrecked. They feel lost, alone and without any real hope of rescue. Any sense of normalcy in our lives has gone by the wayside. Maybe you have been cooped up at home, or your job prospects have gone dim. Perhaps you or your family has been directly impacted health wise by the virus.

Even simple things like going to the movies are no longer happening. Going to the ice cream parlor is an adventure all in itself because of safety concerns. And for most of us the biggest issue is the **shutdown of our churches.** As a nation we have come to rely on the 'in person' touch & sense of belonging that comes during those weekly services. There is no way to sugarcoat our feelings of being shipwrecked.

So back to the Billy Graham shipwrecked guy who lost everything when his hut burned down. About an hour later a **rescue boat** came up on shore. The shipwrecked guy was absolutely amazed. For months there had been absolutely no sign of life out on the horizon. Yet just an hour after he lost everything, he is saved. He asked his rescuers what made them stop and come ashore. They said in a very matter of fact way, *'Well, we saw your rescue fire & we knew someone needed help.'*

What was Billy Graham trying to tell us with this story? Could it be that no matter how bad things look in our lives **(like Covid-19),** God is still on the job and will find a way out for you???

In the book of Hebrews it says, *'I will NEVER leave you or forsake you.'* Are times tough right now? You betcha! Are we all feeling <u>more</u> than just a little shipwrecked? Yes, we are! Can you see a rescue ship on the horizon? Probably <u>not!</u> The Good News is that God has **<u>NOT</u>** forgotten us. He is still on the throne, and he will use any means necessary to rescue you!

The same God that miraculously parted the Red Sea is still alive & well & knows how to get things done! The same God that knocked down the Walls of Jericho is still right here with us and will knock down your walls.

The same God that sent his son Jesus to save us is still on the throne and still wants to save you. Yes, we are going thru the fire right now with Covid-19, but remember the fire is **<u>NOT</u>** our final destination! With the Lord guiding us, we will get thru to the other side! Do you need to be rescued??? If so just remember...

God will rescue
you, even if he has
to burn down
your <u>hut</u> to do it!

A champion is someone who gets up when he can't. Quote by boxing great Jack Dempsey

19
Bring It On!!!

Have you ever watched a Heavy Weight Boxing Match? It's a battle between two incredibly big, strong, powerful, and talented individuals. Think *Muhammed Ali, Joe Frazier, Mike Tyson, George Foreman, Jack Dempsey & many more!* Most of the time these heavy weight fights are not pretty. It's usually two guys at the peak of their physical powers going at each other with only one purpose—Knock the other guy out! They call these knock out punches—**Haymakers!**

Fast forward to current date! From a Pastor's perspective I'm seeing a current day battle of the heavyweights. In one corner wearing the **Red Trunks** is a guy with a powerful right hook—his name is **Satan.** The Bible tells us that Satan is a liar, a deceiver and like a roaring lion seeking to devour. And oh baby, has he been living up to his reputation lately. Think the worst pandemic in more than **100 years!** Think this most recent Texas winter storm which is ranking as the worst in the past **100 years!** Think the incredible divisiveness which seems to be gripping our nation! *It seems like Satan has been on a roll lately.*

But of course, it takes **two** fighters to have a heavyweight fight. In the other corner wearing the **Blue Heavenly Trunks** is a guy with his own powerful right hook—his name is **Jesus!!!** The Bible tells us that Jesus is all about Love, Caring & Compassion. Even more important he is all about salvation—**our Salvation!**

How about you? Are you feeling like you are in your own heavyweight battle?

Think pandemic! There is no way to sugarcoat the fact that the **COVID-19 pandemic** has hit our nation hard. And while every country on the planet has been impacted, in the United States alone there has been over **TWENTY SEVEN MILLION Covid-19** cases along with a staggering **550,000+** deaths. Unemployment has been up to **15%** & families; businesses & churches are struggling just to survive.

Or how about this latest winter storm which many are calling the worst in the last **100 years.** Along with the bitter cold, millions have lost power, creating life threatening situations. And far too many have died or been injured on iced covered highways. At last count more than 200 people died because of this winter storm. And millions more have been hit hard financially by this once in a lifetime storm.

The **SoupMobile** has not been spared from this titanic heavyweight battle. Like many charities we have been hit hard by the pandemic. Only by God's grace have we managed to stay open every single day since the pandemic started. Only by his grace have we been able to meet the increased demand for our feeding services to the homeless & needy children in Dallas, Texas.

And just like you, this winter storm of a lifetime has hit us hard. Again, by God's grace we've remained open but then out of

the blue *Satan hit us with a haymaker.*
Even after taking careful precautions, the
pipes in **SoupMobile Church** froze
Wednesday night (Feb. 17th) and we had a
flood of epic proportions. **Think Noah's
Ark!** The water damage was beyond what
one could imagine. No doubt about it, Satan
does seem to be on a roll!

Now the question for all of us is what are we
going to do? As a Pastor I would say first
and foremost that you need to *pick a side.
Which heavyweight are you going to place
your bet on?* Will it be **Satan**--one of the
most powerful heavyweights of all time OR
will it be **Jesus**---the one who gave up his
life on the Cross for you!

In the book of Corinthians, it says: *'Thanks
be to God; He gives us victory through
Jesus Christ.'* Yes, you gotta pick a side.
You gotta pick who you will follow!

Jesus himself told us that *'In the world you
will have tribulation but take heart; I have
overcome the world.'* And yes, we are all
having tribulation right now. Think

pandemic; think winter storm; think pipes freezing and flooding SoupMobile Church.

I will tell you what I tell my congregation at SoupMobile Church, I don't care what Satan throws at us. Pandemics; winter storms; flooded church; or even the kitchen sink – **BRING IT ON!** We are picking Jesus in this battle of the Titans and sticking with HIM – No Matter What! I urge you to do the same! HE will not fail you. I leave you with these words from the book of Joshua:

'As for me and my household, we will serve the LORD.'

Courage is being scared to death &
saddling up anyway!
Quote by John Wayne

20

Gunfight at the O.K. Corral

We've all watched the story of the Gunfight at the O.K. Corral on TV or at the Movies. Did you know that it's a **true story** that actually took place on **October 26, 1881.**

It was a stressful time in American history!

As the old saying goes, 'The times they were a-changing.' The United States was experiencing a **massive migration** from the East Coast all the way to California.

The Old West was changing with a mix of the *old cowboy way of life and the new ways brought by the Easterners.*

The actual Gunfight takes place in the town Tombstone, Arizona in the fall of **1881.**

Back in 1881 Tombstone had numerous fancy Restaurants, **#1** Bowling Alley, **#1** Ice Cream parlor, **#1** Icehouse, **#1** School, **#1** Opera House, **#2** Banks, **#3** Newspapers, **#4** Churches...

& more than **#100** saloons!!!

The gunfight was between **Wyatt Earp** & his deputies against the bad guys led by the **Clanton brothers.**

It was over in a **mere 30 seconds** with Wyatt & his sidekicks winning the battle. Fast forward to current date. Much like 1881, our country is going thru a stressful time with the COVID-19 pandemic, worst winter storm in the last 100 years, business & churches trying to survive and families struggling to keep their heads above water.

In many ways we are having our own Gunfight at the O.K. Corral as we fight thru these difficult issues.

The difference is that unlike the 1881 gunfight that was over in 30 seconds, the one we are in now seems never ending.

Wyatt won his gunfight with a fast draw and steady hand. The question we are facing today is how are we going to win our own gunfight???

The answer comes from a book that was written thousands of years ago. You know the book I'm talking about—the **Bible!**

Some say that the **Bible** is outdated because times have changed since Jesus walked the earth. Let me give you my take on this as a Pastor & as someone who follows history.

It is true that we are living in a different age. We live in a time of cars, airplanes, computers, cell phones & space travel. Jesus didn't have to deal with any of that.

However, if you think about it, the troubles we have today are the same as the ones from back then. Just like in the ancient past we still have *Financial, Health & Relationship problems.*

Just like back then we still have Gunfights at our **own** O.K Corral. Yes, we've got problems, but the good news is that we've

GOT ANSWERS & those answers are all in that BOOK from thousands of years ago.

In the Book of James, it says: **'Consider it pure joy, my brothers & sisters, whenever you face trials, because you know that the testing of your faith produces perseverance. Let perseverance finish its work so that you may be mature & complete, not lacking anything.'** Or to put it in simpler terms, think of the motto of weightlifters in the gym when they say, **'NO PAIN, NO GAIN.'**

Yes, we are going thru painful times! Yes, times are stressful. And yes 'the times, *they are a-changing.'* However, God is using these tough times to build our faith and draw us closer to HIM.

God promises us that he will *'work out all things together for the good.'* Today, much like the Gunfight at the O.K. Corral in 1881, the bullets are flying, and people are hurting.

The good news is that just like Wyatt & his deputies, **we will win this gunfight.** We will build our faith and our walk with the Lord will be closer than anything we could have ever imagined.

We will win this gunfight because the Lord has promised that *'He will never leave or forsake us.'* He has promised that he will fight for us! He promises to stand with us, just like he did with Moses, with Joshua, with King David and so many more. I will leave you with the final verse from the Book of Romans: **IF GOD BE FOR US, WHO CAN BE AGAINST US!**

I tell you, whatever you did for one of the least of these Brothers & Sisters, you did for me!
Matthew 25:40

21
Pop Quiz!

Pop Quiz Question: What do you celebrate when you **'get it'** and then you also celebrate when you **get rid of it???**

Pop Quiz Answer: A Home Mortgage!

Our lives are much like that home mortgage. We celebrate the birth of a child with great fanfare and then at his/her passing, our family & friends typically have a **'Celebration of Life'** service. At least we hope they will be celebrating our life and all of our accomplishments!

How about you??? When your life has come to an end, what will your family & friends say? *More importantly what will God say?*

When you look back on your life, will you see pain, mistakes, and heartache? Or will you look back on a life of fulfillment, whereby you filled every moment with proud accomplishments and good deeds?

If you are like most of us, *the answer lies somewhere in between.* Yes, you have done some 'not so good' stuff that you deeply regret & would like to forget. On the other hand, you have also done some good things that you hope your friends & family will reminisce about and you also hope God will take notice of.

However, for many of us, we simply *haven't done enough good things* that we can hang our hat on. And why don't we have enough good things to put on our list? The answer to that question is in the **BOOK!** It says we are *'All sinners & fall short of the glory of God.'* Jesus said that the two greatest commandments are to *'Love the Lord with all your heart AND to Love your neighbor as thyself.'*

The first one about loving the Lord seems to be the easier one for us. It's that second one that we seem to have the most trouble with. Just think about the incredibly divisive world we are living in. People are at each other's throats with anger, bitterness and even violence. They seem to be looking for any excuse to trash one another. We seem to be hating our neighbor—<u>not</u> loving them as ourselves!

Jesus is trying to tell us that if you want your final **'Celebration of Life'** to be a good one, you need to lead a life where you are blessing people (your neighbor) on a regular basis. Not just once in a while, but often!

How often you ask??? How often do I need to bless my fellow man? How about every single day of your life! Yes, you heard right! You need to bless your fellowman *EVERY SINGLE DAY OF YOUR LIFE!*

Oh, I can hear some of you saying, **NO WAY** to that every single day thing! My life is already incredibly busy & I don't have the time. Or maybe you are thinking, gee whiz God, my own life is a mess, and I simply don't have anything to give right now, let alone 'every single day.' And if this is what

you are thinking, you definitely need to
THINK AGAIN!

Let Jesus be your guide in this blessing
others 'every single day thing.' Now I get it
that HE sets a high bar, but you need not be
discouraged. There are plenty of wonderful
things you can do to bless your neighbor
EVERY SINGLE DAY!

You can be a blessing to others by
speaking kind words, a warm smile,
volunteering in your community,
giving to charity, sharing things, giving
food, sharing your testimony, praying
for someone in need or giving someone
a listening ear. You could do at least
one of these things *EVERY SINGLE
DAY* of your life!

-

-

Pop Quiz: Could we change the world overnight if every single person on the Planet did one good deed every single day???

Pop Quiz Answer:

OH BABY, YOU BETTER BELIEVE IT!!!

HE is Risen, but of course!!!

22
Easter Has Been Cancelled --Not!

If Satan had his way Easter would be cancelled. How do we know that? *Check out what the Bible says in 1 Peter 5:8 'Be sober, be vigilant; because your adversary the devil walks about like a roaring lion, seeking whom he may devour.'*

Satan does **not** want us celebrating Easter. I'm not talking about the commercialized Easter whereby we have Easter egg hunts, the Easter Bunny, or an Easter Parade. Those are all fine activities but the real Easter that Satan wants to destroy is the one that is also called **Resurrection Sunday.** This is the Easter day that we celebrate the resurrection of Jesus himself.

All of Christianity is based on the resurrection of Jesus. If Jesus did **not** rise from the dead, *then it's all for naught.* If Jesus did **not** rise after 3 days, then he becomes just **another** Rabbi. Yes, a Rabbi who performed miracles but a Rabbi who could not overcome the ultimate challenge, death itself. So, you better believe that Satan wants Easter to be cancelled. Beyond that he is set on making your life miserable!

Look no further than the story of **Job** to underscore this point. Let's be frank, *lately Satan seems to be on a roll.* Think about it, in the last 15 months since the pandemic began, Satan has done some heavy damage. There have been more than 500,000 Covid-19 deaths in the United States alone; record unemployment, the misery of isolation & a nation that seems to be more divided than ever before. Satan is surely laughing at us.

Satan has won—Right??? **Wrong!** Yes, Satan is having his moment in the sun, but it won't last. He will **not** have the last laugh. How can I say this with such complete confidence? Because I have a Book. It's a history book, a guidebook, a book that offers victory. It's an old book and was written well before any of our current generation lived on this planet. In spite of its ancient heritage, there is real wisdom and truth throughout in its pages.

More important, there is **victory** in the pages of the Book. And yes, this Book is just as relevant today as it was when it was written thousands of years ago. Of course, we are talking about the Bible and in this book, it says in *James 4:7 'Therefore submit to God. Resist the devil and he will flee from you.'*

Easter is **<u>NOT</u>** cancelled. You may not be celebrating it this year quite like in the past, but the celebration in your heart cannot be silenced. We celebrate this Easter with the absolute conviction that Jesus was crucified but rose again the third day & conquered death.

Matthew 28: 6 says it all:
HE IS RISEN!

These momentous words spoken in the book of Matthew by an Angel on Easter morning may be the most significant words ever spoken. Jesus had indeed died on the Cross but had now **conquered** death. And by doing so, a new day of hope has dawned for all of us who believe in HIM. There is no sugarcoating the fact that it's been a rough patch for the last 15 months. Our city, our state, our nation and yes, the entire world has been going thru some real trials. *Yes, Satan has had his moment in the sun, but it won't last.* Remember God's promise that 'HE works out all things together for the good' – even bad things like pandemics!

HE IS RISEN,

EASTER HAS

<u>NOT</u>

BEEN

CANCELLED!!!

1930's Depression-era
'Shanty Towns'

23

Brother Can You Spare a Dime?

The saying 'Brother Can You Spare a Dime' originated back in the 1930's. After the Wall Street crash of 1929, the country was in the midst of the **Great Depression.** Unemployment hit a staggering rate of **25%.** #1 of #4 able bodied citizens could not find a job.

Foreclosure rates hit all-time highs and hundreds of thousands of people lost their homes and ended up living in **'Shanty Towns.'** These were makeshift shacks with no heat or plumbing. Some of the shacks were made from orange crates and one family with children lived in an old piano box.

Birthrates fell dramatically across the country because families simply could not afford another mouth to feed.

Compounding matters was the *failure of more than 5,000 banks.* And just when you thought things couldn't get any worse, many sections of the country were hit by a massive drought that helped spawn the *Great Dust Bowl of the 1930's.*

Hunger was a constant companion and soup lines were a common sight. An entire middle class fell from grace and literally had to beg for food.

Hence the line, **'Brother Can You Spare a Dime.'** How much was a dime worth back then??? A cup of coffee was .5 cents; a loaf of bread .9 cents; and a pound of hamburger was .13 cents.

The question many of our generation now ask is just how did they get thru the 'Great Depression' which lingered on from late 1929 to the start of World War 2 in 1941?

The simple answer to this question is that people stuck together back then!

During the Great Depression, many people showed great kindness to strangers who were down on their luck. People often gave food, clothing, and a place to stay to the needy. Families helped other families and shared resources. They watched out for each other and made it a point to stick together. A winning concept to be sure!

Gee, I wonder where this concept of 'sticking together' came from? *Could it be from the Bible that says:* 'Love thy neighbor as thyself.' This concept seems to be a little out of favor in today's world. I wasn't alive yet when the Great Depression hit, but my 'late' parents were. They told me that as hard and difficult as things were, that people back *then really bought into the concept of helping their neighbor.*
Nowadays it seems like we are at each other's throats. I can't remember a time in my own lifetime where our nation has been

more divisive. Today there seems to be too much <u>hate</u>, too much <u>anger</u> and too much <u>violence</u> in our country.

We live in a **'gotcha'** society and look for reasons to attack our fellowman. Things like civility, understanding, forgiveness and just plain old common decency seem to have fallen by the wayside. **I say enough is enough!** I say we need to return to our roots! Maybe take a page out of the playbook from people who went thru the Great Depression. I say we need to start listening to that guy from 2,000 years ago who said to 'Love thy neighbor as thyself.'

The words of Jesus should be <u>**No.#1**</u> in our lives, whether we are living in the Great Depression or the great Covid-19 pandemic of 2020-2021. You can be a **blessing** to **others** by speaking kind words, volunteering in your community, giving to charity, sharing things, giving food, praying for someone in need or just giving a listening ear to someone.

We need to change the dialogue in our country, and we need to do it now. We need to treat each other with just plain old common decency and kindness. Don't wait for others to make the first move. We need to all rise up and pay forward the Love that Jesus showed us on the Cross more than 2,000 years ago. In the 1930's it was 'Brother can you spare a dime.' In the 2020's lets update that to say:

BROTHER CAN YOU

SPARE SOME LOVE,

SOME KINDNESS,

SOME CIVILITY,

SOME HELP,

SOME UNDERSTANDING

& SOME LOVING YOUR

NEIGHBOR AS YOURSELF!

Time to pump the Brakes!!!

24
Pump the Brakes!

I grew up in Detroit, Michigan. A city that was once called 'The Car Capital of the World.' Back then there weren't so many car companies. The **Big #3** car companies were **Ford, General Motors & Chrysler.**

In many ways the Detroit & Michigan economy was fueled by the production & sales of cars. In fact, cars were how I paid my way thru college. Every summer during my 4 years of college, *I proudly worked on the assembly line at GM's Pontiac Motors.*

It was back then that I first heard the term, **'Pump the Brakes.'** Modern cars have something called ABS—Anti Lock Braking System. In essence the car will **'automatically'** pump the brakes for you to help the car slow down safely & also perform better on slippery surfaces.

But back in my college days, ABS had not been invented yet and drivers were taught to **manually 'pump their brakes'.** I clearly remember many a time driving on the icy roads of Detroit, pressing & releasing my foot on the brake pedal to keep control of the car.

Life can be much like the braking system on a car. Sometimes we need to pump the brakes, but unlike modern cars, our lives do NOT have an automatic braking system. We have to *manually pump the brakes on our own lives,* but in many ways, it's become a lost art.

Back in my college days, life seemed to be simpler, slower paced and sometimes a touch like the town of **Mayberry** in the old Andy Griffith TV show. Today it's all changed. We live in a society very much the opposite of Mayberry. We live in a country that is filled with too much hate, too much anger and too much violence. Crime is on the rise & drug use is off the charts. We live in a *'gotcha'* society & we seem to look for reasons to attack our fellowman. *It's time for all of us to 'Pump the Brakes' on how we are living our lives.*

Let's start with how we drive our cars. Ever drive home at rush hour?
You are taking your life in your own hands. People drive like maniacs. They will cut off their own grandmother to save a few seconds of driving time. And God forbid you are the lead car at a Red light & it turns green, and you don't take off right away. The driver behind you is going to hit their horn big time. And don't get me started on tailgating!

How about 'Pumping the Brakes' on how we treat our fellowman. What's happened to those old-fashioned values like civility, courtesy, grace, patience, and just plain old common decency. When did we forget how to 'reasonably disagree?' *REASONABLY disagree* being the key word's here!

We seem to look at our neighbor in the most contentious way possible. You think I'm exaggerating???

Just look at the incredible divide and divisiveness between our political parties. Both sides are equally judgmental and treat each other with a high level of hostility. Any concept of working together seems to have fallen by the wayside.

We also need to 'Pump the Brakes' on some of the *words that come out of our mouths.* Far too many of the words I hear today are well beyond vile & hateful.

In the book of Proverbs, it says that there is *'Power of Life & Death in the tongue.'* We need to start speaking life to our fellowman, even if we don't agree with everything they say or do.

Jesus hit on this point 2,000 years ago when he said to 'Love thy neighbor as thyself.'

LET'S PUMP
THE BRAKES
ON HATE,
ANGER &
VIOLENCE &
LET'S PUMP UP
THE VOLUME
ON LOVE,
CARING &
COMPASSION!!!

'When the righteous cry for help, the LORD hears & delivers them out of all their troubles.' The Book of Psalms

25
Letter to Jesus!

Dear Jesus,

We need your help down here! It looks as if the world has gone mad. It seems that whatever can go wrong is going wrong. I mean like, check it out! We are going thru the worst pandemic in the last **100 years!** Millions have died and many more millions have suffered. It is true that vaccines offer some real hope, but we aren't out of the woods yet—not by a longshot.

And what about this crazy weather stuff. Some say it's because of global warming and it's for sure that *floods, hurricanes, tornadoes, fires & natural disasters are wreaking havoc on our nation.*

And then there is that 'not getting along with our neighbor thing.' Oh boy, **have we blown it there!** Oh sure, you said in that book from 2,000 years ago that 'We should love our neighbor as ourselves', *but we didn't think you actually meant it.*

Gee whiz Jesus, are you really saying we should love people that have a different skin color, different belief system, different values and horror of horrors don't vote for the same candidates we do? **Really Jesus? Really???**

And my gosh Jesus, did you even know about the internet back in the olden days? Did you even know we would have something called Social Media, and that *with just a few keystrokes on our cellphones we could spew words of hate, anger & threats of violence*. Huh Jesus, did you even know about this Social Media stuff way back then???

In so many ways we are going thru dark times! Of course, Jesus, what would you know about dark times! After all you are sitting pretty, high up there in heaven on the right-hand side of God himself. What would you know about the problems we are having down here on this planet?

OH WAIT!!! **Hold the phone!** Now that I think about it, you do know a thing or two about dark times. You were born in the darkness, right? You came to us on the **nightshift.** The three wise men followed a star in the darkness to find you. Even as a baby you felt the darkness of the world. Remember King Herod? He wanted you dead so badly that he went on a rampage killing babies.

It didn't get much better for you as an adult. *While thousands loved you, many hated you.* Remember the Pharisees? Or how about that Judas guy? Or how about the darkness of the Cross. *Whew, now that I think about it, you do indeed know a thing or two about the dark & divisive world that we are living in.*

So, who better to come to for help than you! **You've been there, done that!** Now I know we have blown it—Bigtime! We've strayed so far from you that we've made the

Prodigal Son *look like a Choir Boy.* Over the past **50+** years we have taken God out of our schools, our businesses, our courts & our public institutions.

And unbelievably, we've even said the Ten Commandments are not suitable for public display. Is there any wonder we are in the mess we are in. Jesus, you are our only hope in getting out of this fix we've landed in!

We've burned all of our bridges & we've got nowhere else to turn—except to you! I/We confess and repent of our sins.

We humbly ask you to take us back! Please Lord, forgive us & heal our land! What will be the answer to our plea???
Check out the answer on the next page:

2 Chronicles 7:14

If my people, who are called by my name, will humble themselves and pray and seek my face and turn from their wicked ways, then I will hear from heaven, and I will forgive their sin and will heal their land.

**Love one another, as I
have Loved you!
John 13:34**

26
Love One Another!

As a Pastor I get lots of questions! However, the most common question I get in some form is, **'What is the meaning of life?'**

Basically, people want to know why they were even born? Why are they even on the planet? What are they supposed to do with their lives? **What's it all about?**

I remember as a child growing up in Detroit, Michigan, I dreamed about growing up to be a cowboy, an astronaut, a movie star or maybe even President of the United States. *Like many people, I thought the 'meaning of life' was based on what I became.*

For example, Michael Jordan is one of the best <u>basketball</u> players ever; or Jack Nicklaus being a fantastic <u>golfer;</u> or maybe someone becomes a famous <u>chef;</u> a Nobel prize-winning <u>writer;</u> a <u>Nurse;</u> a <u>Doctor</u> or how about a great <u>teacher?</u>

In other words, most people see the 'meaning of life' **in direct proportion to what they have accomplished.** For them, those accomplishments answer the question, what's the meaning of life, why was I born and what's it all about!

I think it's admirable to have goals. I think it's wonderful to have **dreams & aspirations.** And while my childhood dreams did **NOT** become a reality, I did go on to attain some other modest successes in life, not the least of which was becoming a Pastor. More about that later!

However, I would humbly submit that those successes are <u>NOT</u> the 'meaning of life.' **Not for me and not for you!** The successes and accomplishments of your life are only the **<u>springboard</u>** for you to live out the real meaning of life.

What is the real meaning of life? What is your purpose in life? Why are you even on the planet? What's it all about? The answer is <u>not</u> complicated and lies in three simple words: ***LOVE ONE ANOTHER!***

Yes folks, that's it! The reason you were even born is to 'Love one another.' What you have accomplished in life is just the platform, the springboard, the catalyst to 'Love one another.'

In my own case, God called me to be a Pastor. This in spite of the fact that I am the most un-qualified person on the planet to be a Pastor. Nonetheless I use my Pastor platform to honor those words: 'Love one another.'

But you can use virtually any platform to do the same. A teacher can do it, a writer, a golfer, a home maker, Nurse, Doctor, etc. Your life successes and accomplishments can be your own personal platform to spread love in your own little corner of the world.

We are living in some crazy times right now. Our nation is divided like it's never been before. This divisiveness runs along many fronts, including political, religious, color, race, etc. By any measurement there is too much hate, too much anger and too much violence.

There are #13 separate & distinct times in the Bible where it says, 'Love one another.' The actual word Love appears more than **300 times** in the Bible. God set the ultimate example for all of us when it comes to Love. It says in John 3:16 *'For God so Loved the world that he gave his only begotten son.'* Then Jesus showed his immense Love for us by dying on the Cross. It's really all about Love! What higher purpose can there be! Love is the great restorer, the ultimate healer & the salve for every wound.

QUESTION:

What's the meaning of life???

ANSWER: LOVE ONE ANOTHER!!!

**Be kind to one another,
tenderhearted, forgiving
one another!
The Book of Ephesians**

27
Be Kind

In recent years, it seems that our nation has become increasingly *fractured & divided.* It goes well beyond just Democrat/Republican bickering. We seem to be divided on issues regarding race, religion, creed, gender & so much more. *We can't seem to agree on anything!*

As a Pastor, I'm **NOT** really too concerned about this lack of agreement. It's not crucial that we agree on everything. My late father taught me that '*It's okay to disagree with others as long as we REASONABLY DISAGREE*'. And as simple and profound as that statement is, we don't seem to have a clue on how to 'reasonably disagree' with our fellow man. We've become an **'all or nothing'** culture. If we don't agree with someone, we attack them. We have developed something called **'cancel culture.'** If we don't agree with someone's beliefs, words, or actions, we literally try to destroy them, ruin their reputation, get them fired from their jobs & harass them into utter oblivion.

It wasn't always like this. As a child growing up in Detroit, Michigan we actually experienced a kinder, gentler America. Yes, people disagreed back then, *but they did it with a touch of grace, class & understanding*. The good news is that all is NOT lost. We can get back to that kinder, gentler time. And we don't have to wait to do it.

Let's start right now by treating each other with a kind word, a smile, a pat on the back or a listening ear. We can even pray for each other. And we can do all of this for our fellow man, EVEN IF WE DISAGREE WITH THEM.

Sounds radical huh! But guess what, it's totally doable! How about we flat out reject this concept called 'cancel culture.' How about we stop trying to harass our neighbor into oblivion when we disagree with them. *If each one of us would do a simple act of kindness every day, we could change the world.*

I'm not asking you to cure cancer, solve global warming or fix the troubles of the entire world. All I'm asking is that you start being kind to your fellowman—your neighbor. The Dalai Lama said, "Be kind whenever possible." And then he followed that up by saying: "It is always possible." Now that's *simple & profound.*

Let's reject this cancel culture concept & replace it with some simple acts of kindness. *Things like smiles, listening ears, kind words, volunteering, and of course prayers are all indeed always possible!*

And if we are to have any semblance of a 'cancel culture', let's have one where we cancel hate, cancel anger, cancel bitterness, cancel vengeance, and cancel violence.

Do you remember the late George H.W. Bush? On August 18, 1988, he received his party's nomination for President of the United States. In his acceptance speech, he called for a **"kinder, gentler nation."**

He wasn't speaking as a Republican, Democrat or Liberal. He was speaking as a father, husband, friend, Believer, and citizen of our great nation. His words were also *simple & profound.*

Let's hold true to the words spoken by Jesus himself more than 2,000 years ago. *"Love thy neighbor as thyself.*" Oh baby, now that's **simple & profound.** Let's learn from the **simple & profound** words of these four-amazing people!

1. <u>*My Late Father:*</u> *"Lets reasonably disagree."*

2. <u>*The Dalai Lama:*</u> *"Be kind whenever possible. It is always possible."*

3. <u>*George H.W. Bush:*</u> *"A kinder, gentler nation."*

4. <u>*Jesus:*</u> *"Love thy neighbor as thyself."*

LET'S ALL JUST BE KIND!!!

SoupMan stooping down to help one of the ones Jesus calls the 'least of these.'

28

Stoop Down!

Right from birth, parents of all nations, races, creeds & religious persuasions are hoping to put their children on the *fast track to success*. For most it all starts with schooling. When I was growing up in Detroit, Michigan, all we had was **basic Kindergarten** for children around 5-6 years old.

Then over the years something new came along called **Prekindergarten** (Pre-K) for children 4 -5 years old. But even that wasn't enough & along came **Pre-School** for children starting as early as 2 years old. All in hopes of giving our children a head start in life. I would suggest to you that trying to give children a head start in this world is perfectly acceptable. **It's more than Okay!** And if all goes well, kids will get caught up (and participate) in their parents' efforts to make them successful. Kids will then start to develop their own dreams for a successful life.

When I was growing up, I dreamed about being a cowboy, an astronaut, a movie star or maybe even President of the United States. **Did I achieve any of those dreams? No, I did NOT!** However, I did become a Pastor, in spite of the fact that I am the most un-qualified person on the PLANET to be a Pastor.

This me becoming a Pastor paradox, mystery, conundrum & brain-teaser is explained in: *Isaiah 55:8 'For my thoughts are not your thoughts, neither are your ways my ways, saith the Lord.'*

So, what might success look like for your children??? Are you hoping they will be a cowboy, an astronaut, a movie star or maybe even the

President of the United States? Perhaps you want them to be a professor, a sports star, a President of a large corporation, wealthy financier, Doctor, Nurse, Nobel Prize winner, *or maybe even a PASTOR!* Whatever your goal, most parents only want the best for their children. They hope/pray that their children will enjoy great success, joy & happiness in their lives.

As a Pastor I've got my own ideas on what should be the **Number #1** thing parents dream about as regards success for their children. Let me preface this by saying that I am humbly remembering that I am the most un-qualified person on the Planet to be a Pastor. However, if anyone has an issue with that, they will have to take it up with God. Being a Pastor was definitely <u>NOT</u> my idea—**God thought that one up all on his own!**

So back to what I believe should be the **Number #1** thing we aspire for our children. And we should start doing this before **Kindergarten,** before **Pre-K,** before **Pre-School** & even before they are born. I believe we should teach our children how to **STOOP DOWN.** Yes, you heard right--Stoop down!

I remember once telling this to a parent who came to me for pastoral counseling about some issues he was having with his child. He _**howled**_ when I told him he should teach his child to stoop down. He said he was trying to do just the opposite and to teach his child to rise up and be successful—**NOT stoop down!** Well after the dust settled, I explained what I meant.   I quoted the words of Henry Van Dyke who said: **"There is a loftier ambition than merely to stand high in the world.** _It is to 'stoop down' and lift mankind a little higher."_ Oh baby, now those are insightful words. Henry Van Dyke was saying it's okay to strive for success but to use that success to 'stoop down' & help others.

Jesus was the master of 'Stooping Down' to help others. The Bible **tells us that the mission of Christ was** to reach out to the poor, to deliver the captives, to restore sight to the blind, and to lift up the downtrodden. This mission is as relevant today as it was then. We should commit ourselves to fulfilling this mission. Let's teach and encourage everyone *(not just our children)* to strive to be successful in life AND then to...

STOOP DOWN!!!

29
WarGames

The movie War-Games came out in **1983** and starred Matthew Broderick who plays David Lightman, a young computer hacker who unwittingly accesses a United States military supercomputer that is programmed to **predict & execute nuclear war against the Soviet Union.**

Broderick initiates *(what he thinks is a game)* of Global Thermonuclear War, playing as the <u>Soviet Union</u> and begins targeting American cities. He has no idea that the supercomputer known as WOPR (pronounced 'whopper') is actually playing the game for **'real.'**

WOPR's goal is to launch a real nuclear strike against Russia. All the while Broderick thinks *it's just a computer 'game.'* The U.S. supercomputer WOPR does <u>not</u>

understand the difference between *reality and simulation*. WOPR's only goal is to 'win the game' by launching **real nuclear missiles** and obliterating the Soviet Union. However, the good news is that the computer is self-adaptive and has the ability to learn. At the last moment, just before WOPR actually launches the very real U.S. nuclear missiles, it learns the lesson and says in one of the most famous movie lines of all time: *Nuclear war is a 'strange game' in which the only winning move is <u>NOT</u> to play.*

In many ways our lives are played out just like the movie **WarGames!** Like Matthew Broderick, we don't take things seriously enough! In some ways, we think it's *all just a game* and that there aren't really any consequences—well, at least no <u>immediate consequences!</u>

For example, we might get hooked on **drugs or alcohol.** We don't worry too much about it because we figure we can stop anytime we want. But by the time we do want to stop, it can often be **_too late!_**

Or how about where the Bible tells us in the Book of Acts to **'Believe in the Lord Jesus Christ & thou shalt be saved.'** All too many think that there's no hurry accepting Jesus. After all, they have plenty of time left before their passing---**or do they???** In the Book of Job, it says **'Man's days are determined by God.'** Before we know it, it might just be too late to accept Jesus as our Lord & Savior. **It's not a _game!_**

Now you may be saying, hey Pastor, you're certainly **not** talking about me. I don't _abuse drugs or alcohol_ & I accepted Jesus long ago. Okay, good for you, but how high do you score on this next question??? **_Are_** *you, have you been, or do you plan to start Loving thy neighbor as thyself???*

Now let's all be **honest** here! No fudging & no sweeping this under the rug. Remember it was Jesus himself who said the two greatest commandments are to *'Love the Lord thy God with all thy heart AND to Love thy neighbor as thyself.'* So, this is big stuff here, it comes right from the man himself---Jesus!!! Are you really loving thy neighbor or *just tolerating him?*

Ask yourself, are you really loving your neighbor that doesn't <u>vote</u> like you; doesn't <u>pray</u> like you; doesn't <u>speak</u> like you; doesn't <u>love</u> like you; doesn't <u>think</u> like you & doesn't <u>look</u> like you??? Really, how are you doing on all the above? Be honest—**at least with yourself.** If you are like most of us, you *aren't cutting the mustard in* some of the above areas. And remember it's not enough to be neutral. Jesus was telling us to be proactive when he said to Love your neighbor as thyself. This is NOT a game like in the movie WarGames. Someday *(even when we get to heaven),* we will still have to answer for our actions on this planet.

It's not too late for you to get it all together. It's not too late to start loving your neighbor regardless of his *race, creed, gender, color, religion, or political persuasion.* Start with kind words, warm smiles, volunteering, giving, sharing, listening & by gosh you could even pray for your neighbor.

YES, PRAY FOR THAT NEIGHBOR WHO IS NOTHING LIKE YOU!!!

The Greenland Shark— will it live forever?

30
SHARKS!

This is a real picture of a **394** year old Greenland Shark that was recently discovered in the Arctic Ocean. He's been calmly and confidently *wandering the ocean since 1627.* He's at the top of the food chain so he has little to worry about. For this shark, life is good!!!

When I first heard about the age **(almost 400 years old)** of this shark, I said **NO WAY!!!** No way anything could live that long and even if it could, how could anyone say with any certainty what the age was. Well guess what? It seems that scientists can use carbon dating to estimate the **age** of **Greenland** sharks. Inside the **shark**'s eyes, there are proteins that are formed before birth and do not degrade with age, like a fossil preserved in amber. Scientists discovered that they could determine the **age** of the **sharks** by carbon-dating these proteins. Who knew!!!

Oh Baby, if only our own lives were as stable and serene as the Greenland Shark. Alas they are not!

One of my Pastor friends made the comment that we are living in perilous times! In some ways, he was right. Think about it! We are going thru the worst pandemic *in the last 100 years!* Every summer fires rage out of control on much of the West coast of our country. This past February we had a **100-year** winter storm. Every time we pick up the newspaper we read about the increase of crime, drug use and violence in our country. To top it all off, we are a divided country! I'm not just talking about a political divide but literally a country so divisive that we are at *each other's throats.* Hmm, it seems that the cushy life of the Greenland shark is starting to look **pretty good!**

Compounding matters is that the Bible tells us in the Book of John that *we will have tribulation on this earth.* Yikes, even the Bible confirms that sometimes life is going to get a bit bumpy.

It reminds me of the famous movie line by **Bette Davis** in the 1950 movie All About Eve. She says, *"Fasten your seat belts, it's going to be a bumpy night."*

Here's the question many of us are asking: Is there any hope for us, *or is life just gonna be crappy all the time?* Ah Grasshopper, have I got 'good' news for you! No, make that 'great' news! Make that 'wonderful' news! Make that beyond wonderful news! You see, there is this guy who walked the planet about **2,000** years ago! The Bible tells us in the Book of John, *'Be of good cheer for I have overcome the world.'*

But hold your horses, it gets even better. It goes on to say in the Book of John, *'I am come that you might have life, and that you might have it more abundantly.'* And who is that guy from a few thousand years ago??? Jesus, of course! Ah, now we are getting somewhere! Now we are seeing some light at the end of the tunnel! **Now we have some hope!**

The Bible further elaborates on this point. In the Book of Romans, it says that *'God works out ALL things together for the good.'*

I want you all to know that I'm not making light of the problems many of you are facing. What I am saying is that God has got your back! HE's on the job, He Loves you like crazy, and HE will fight for you!

Yes, life can get pretty rough sometimes, but Jesus knows a little about that rough stuff. Remember the **agony of the Cross?**

Oh yeah, Jesus knows a thing or two about our **pain, discouragement,** and **suffering.**

Question: Will our lives ever be as safe, comfortable, and serene as the Greenland shark that is almost 400 years old???

Answer: Nope, afraid not!

However please remember, we have an ace in the hole. We have Jesus! And HE has promised to never leave or forsake us!!!

A Unicorn??? No, it's the cool, hip, mod, rad, chic, stylish, vogue & groovy SoupMobile Donut Car!

31
DONUTS!!!

Lets talk about Donuts! **Yes Donuts!** Oh I can hear you saying, 'Oh my, the Pastor has gone off the deep end—**<u>AGAIN!</u>'** Well maybe so, but before you send me packing, consider the possibility that the Bible refers to donuts in Leviticus 7:12 *'If he offers it for a thanksgiving, then he shall offer with the sacrifice of thanksgiving unleavened cakes mingled with oil, and unleavened wafers anointed with oil, **and cakes mingled with oil, of fine flour, fried.'***

Is it just possible that while the Bible does <u>not</u> use the actual word Donuts, that it does refer to a Donut type product when it says *'Cakes mingled with oil, of fine flour, fried?'* Is it just possible???

So now I can hear you saying, 'Gee whiz Pastor David, why all the fuss about donuts and what's any of this got to do with a mini-sermon? *Okay, so glad you asked!* Here's why all the fuss! Since **2003** the SoupMobile has fed the **homeless** & **needy children** hearty & healthy meals right here in Dallas, Texas. However like most of us they occasionally enjoy a sweet treat and that's where the donuts come in! Donuts are just an expansion of our mission.

And what is that mission? *Feeding the homeless & needy children, you say!!!* **NO! NO! NO!** Feeding the homeless & needy children is **not** our primary mission. Oh I know it looks like it is but it's not! Our Number #1 mission is sharing **Love, Caring & Compassion** with the ones Jesus calls the 'least of these.' Yes the food is absolutely and critically important, but its just the *doorway into their hearts.* And on this point we take our cue straight from Jesus himself. Remember the Bible story in the Book of Mark on how Jesus was preaching to the crowds and then he fed them by multiplying the loaves and the fishes. Yes the food was absolutely important *but the Love that Jesus brought to that table was his Number #1 mission.*

So what about you! What's your **Number #1** mission in life? Remember it's <u>not</u> about your career, your education level or your achievements. All of these are important but they are just the doorway into people's hearts.

Your **Number #1 Mission** should be exactly the same as was the mission of Jesus. And that is to bring Love to the world. In this case, your own little corner of the world. Simple but yet so profound, don't you think! How can you bring <u>Love</u> to your corner of the world? Ah **Grasshopper**, there are soooooooooooooo many ways. We can't all be a *Mother Teresa* but you <u>can</u> make a real difference in your own little corner of the world.

You can start with giving people a warm smile, cut your elderly neighbor's grass, put a quarter in a parking meter, buy a burger for a homeless person, pray for someone, give a listening ear, donate to your favorite charity *or even volunteer somewhere!* If you really think about it, there are lots of ways you can bless your fellowman!
If you're thinking you *don't have enough time* then let me quote the words of Jackson Brown: "Don't say you don't have enough time. You have *exactly the same number of hours per day* that were given to Helen Keller, Pasteur, Michelangelo, Mother Teresa, Leonardo da Vinci, Thomas Jefferson, and Albert Einstein."

What do you think???
Can we really use
Donuts to bring Love
to our fellowman?

Well, it seems we can
& my guess is that
Jesus is up there just
looking down with a
small wry smile &
saying....
'Rock on Baby!'

-

Pa, when's Jesus coming back???

32
HE's COMING BACK, BUT WHEN???

In this picture, Opie asks his Pa 'When is Jesus coming back?' Andy answers: 'I don't rightly know. Ya see Opie, you and I are <u>not</u> on the <u>planning</u> committee. *We're on the <u>welcoming</u> committee!'*

Is Jesus coming back? **You betcha!** <u>When</u> is he coming back? Ah, therein lies the *Million Dollar* question! We simply don't know! The Bible tells us in the book of Matthew, *'About that day or hour no one knows...therefore keep watch, because you do not know on what day your Lord will come.'*

This leads to the obvious question, **how are we going to be ready for HIS return if we don't know <u>when</u> he is coming?** On that score the answer is simplicity itself. We can be ready for his return by living our lives the way Jesus says we should. HE said that the two greatest commandments are: *1. Love the Lord thy God with all thy heart! 2. Love thy neighbor as thyself!*

Sounds reasonable, right? Piece of cake, right? No problem, right?

Easy-Peasy, don't you think? Could it really be that simple? Is that all we need to do to get ready for his return? Well almost! There is a **3rd** thing we all need to do. *Accept Jesus as your Lord & Savior!* In the Bible in the Book of Acts, it tells us to 'Believe on the Lord Jesus Christ & thou shalt be saved.'

Interestingly enough, in this simple list of three things to do to be ready for Jesus' return, most of us get **pretty high marks** for No.**#1** & **#3.**

It's that **No.#2** thing about 'Loving thy neighbor as thyself' where we seem to hit the most *speed bumps.* And based on the incredibly divisive world we are currently living in; I'm talking about some giant speed bumps. Think about it! Jesus returns & causally asks you these *#3 key questions.*

1. *Did you Love the Lord thy God with all thy heart?* You shake your head in the affirmative and say a loud & confident **YES!**

2. *Did you Love your neighbor as thyself?* You take a deep breath, start hemming and hawing, cough, stutter just a bit and turn down your head and sheepishly say...**NOT SO MUCH!**

3. *Did you accept me as your Lord & Savior?* This one is easy for you, and you let out a big shout & say a joyous **YES, YES YES!**

Oh Baby, talk about a *speed bump!* Yeah, you got 2 out of 3 but don't be so quick to pat yourself on the back. *2 out of 3* may be great in baseball but in God's world, you missed the mark bigtime when you answered **'Not so much'** on the number two question, *did you Love your neighbor as thyself.* So sorry to say, but in this case, two out of three *just ain't gonna cut it*.

We need to all understand that we are talking about the SECOND GREATEST COMMANDMENT! *'Love your neighbor as thyself.'* This second greatest commandment came from Jesus himself. It can't get any more urgent than that.

We need to get our act together **before** Jesus comes back. Once he's back, it will be too late for you to get your act together!

START GETTING READY NOW! Start loving your neighbor regardless of his race, creed, gender, color, religion, or political persuasion.

Start being a blessing to everyone around you. **START NOW!** You can bless your fellowman in so many ways. **START NOW!**

Start with some kind words, a warm smile, volunteering in your community, giving to charity, sharing things, giving food, sharing your testimony, giving a listening ear, or praying for someone in need. **START NOW!** Time is tight! You need to get your act together right **now,** because guess what, *Jesus is coming back!!!*

AND HE MAY JUST COME BACK TODAY!!!

CONTACT INFORMATION:

Would you like to contact the SoupMan?

If you want to contact
David Timothy, a.k.a. SoupMan,
you can email him at:
david@soupmobile.org

David personally reads all of his
emails, and he makes it a point
to respond to each and every one
of them!

Or you can send a letter to:

SoupMobile

Attn: SoupMan

2490 Coombs St.

Dallas, Texas 75215

VOLUNTEER INFORMATION:

Would you like to volunteer with the SoupMobile?

If so, simply go to **www.soupmobile.org** and click on the red **VOLUNTEER** button & sign up right online.

SUPPORT INFORMATION:

Would you like to support us financially & help us feed the homeless & needy children in Dallas, Texas?

If so, simply go to **www.soupmobile.org** and click on the yellow **DONATE** button for more details.

<u>Do you need Prayer?</u>

If you need prayer for yourself, a family member, a friend or a loved one, simply go to **www.soupmobile.org** and click on **'Need Prayer.'** Our Prayer Team would be honored to pray for you & yours!

<u>Would you like to join our Prayer Team?</u>

If so, simply go to **www.soupmobile.org** and click **'Prayer Team.'**

One last thing...

Publisher's Note:

Question? Did you feel blessed by this book of 5 Minute Mini-Sermons? If you answered yes, please go to **amazon.com** & write a review.

Positive reviews help book sales & Pastor David gives *all of his royalties* from his book sales to the SoupMobile to help feed the homeless & needy children.

He keeps nothing for himself.